SOMET
TO S

GW01185701

MELODY EDITION

I

COMPILED BY

GEOFFREY BRACE

CAMBRIDGE

AT THE UNIVERSITY PRESS

1970

PUBLISHED BY
THE SYNDICS OF THE CAMBRIDGE UNIVERSITY PRESS

Bentley House, 200 Euston Road, London, N.W.1
American Branch: 32 East 57th Street, New York, N.Y. 10022

Standard Book Number: 0 521 04295 X

First published	1963
Reprinted	1964
	1965
	1966
	1968
	1970

Printed in Great Britain by Halstan and Company, Ltd

CONTENTS

ACKNOWLEDGEMENTS

As well as the publishers listed in the note on copyright, I should like to thank the collectors of folk-song material whose work has helped to make this kind of book possible, and in particular A. L. Lloyd, Peter Kennedy and Ewan MacColl, who have kindly answered questions and given permission for material to be used.

I am particularly anxious to record my gratitude to Mr G. O. Richards for advice and help with the accompaniments. Mr Richards has removed awkwardnesses and suggested happy touches; and I believe these two kinds of improvement will give the accompanist pleasure as well as make his task easier.

G. B.

MELBOURN,
CAMBRIDGESHIRE

NOTE

The topmost notes in heavy type are always the melody.

The notes in small type can be sung by a small section of the class or group, or played on suitable instruments.

Another small section of voices or instruments can sing or play the *lower* notes in heavy type.

The time values of the first verse must be changed at the discretion of the singer to fit the words of the other verses.

Ballads

1. THE GYPSY DAVEY

This is one of the many versions of the 'Wraggle Taggle Gypsies' story. It is quite possible that it is based on fact: a lady of high birth may have got tired of waiting at home while her lord was hunting, and been attracted by a handsome, wandering gypsy, begging at the castle gate.

It was late last night when the squire came home and ask - ing for his la - dy.____ The on - ly ans - wer____ that he got, 'She's gone with the Gyp - sy Da - vey, she's gone with the Gyp - sy Da - vey.'

2 'Go saddle for me my buckskin horse
And a hundred dollar saddle.
Point out to me their wagon tracks
And after them I'll travel.'

3 Well he had not rode to the midnight moon
When he saw the campfire gleaming.
He heard the notes of the big guitar
And the noise of the gypsies singing.

4 'Have you forsaken your house and home?
Have you forsaken your baby?
Have you forsaken your husband dear
To go with the Gypsy Davey?'

5 'Yes, I've forsaken my husband dear
To go with the Gypsy Davey,
And I've forsaken my mansion high
But not my blue-eyed baby.'

6 'Take off, take off your buckskin gloves
Made of Spanish leather,
Give to me your lilywhite hand
And we'll ride home together.'

7 'No, I won't take off my buckskin gloves
Made of Spanish leather.
I'll go my way from day to day
And sing with the Gypsy Davey.'

2. TURPIN HERO

Dick Turpin was hanged at York on 10 April 1739, after a successful career as a high-way man round that city.

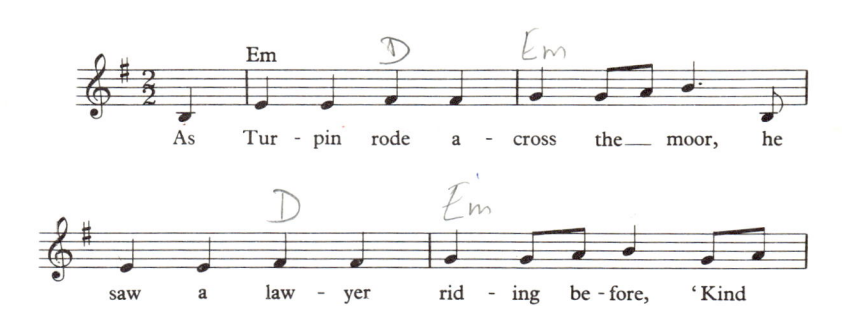

As Tur - pin rode a - cross the — moor, he saw a law - yer rid - ing be - fore, 'Kind

sir,' says he, 'aren't you a - fraid of

Tur - pin, that mis - chie - vous blade?' O Rare

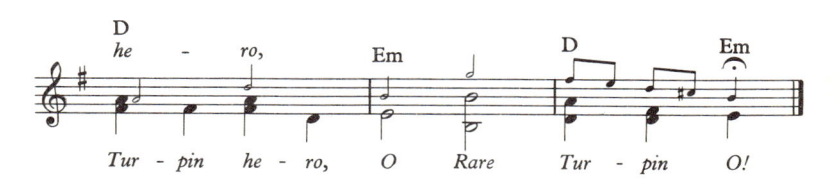

Tur - pin he - ro, O Rare Tur - pin O!

2 Says Turpin, 'He won't find me out.
I've hid my money in my boot.'
The lawyer says 'No one can find
The gold that's stitched in my cape behind.'

3 As they rode by the foot of the hill
Turpin commands him to stand still.
Says he, 'Your cape I must cut off,
For my mare she needs a new saddle cloth.'

4 As Turpin rode o'er Salisbury Plain
He met a judge and all his train.
Then to the judge he did approach
And robbed him as he sat in his coach.

5 For the stealing of a dunghill cock
Turpin now at last is took.
And now he lingers in a jail
Where his ill luck he doth bewail.

6 Now Turpin is condemned to die
And hang upon the gallows high.
His legacy is the hangman's rope
For the stealing of a dunghill cock.

3. THE BOLD 'PRINCESS ROYAL'

This story of an encounter with pirates exists in many versions. 'The Coasts of High Barbary' tells the same tale.

On the fourth day of Au - gust we sail'd from the land in the bold *Prin - cess Roy - al* bound for New - found - land. We had for - ty bright sea - men for a ship's com - pa - ny and bold - ly from the east - ward to the west - ward bore we.

2 We had not been sailing past two days or three,
When a man from the masthead a sail he did see.
She bore down upon us, a fav'ring wind blew,
While under her mizzen black colours she flew.

3 'Good Lord,' cried the captain, 'what shall we do now?
Here comes a bold pirate to rob us I know.'
'Oh no,' cried the Chief Mate, 'that ne'er shall be so,
We'll shake out a reef boys and from her we'll go.'

4 'Come bear up your courses and heave your ship to,
For I have a letter to send home by you.'
'I'll hold up my courses and heave my ship to,
But it shall be in some harbour and not 'longside you.'

5 She chased us to windward for all that long day,
She chased us to windward but could make no way.
For shots she sent frequent to make us to stay
But she hauled up her mainsail and then bore away.

6 'Thank God,' said the Captain, 'the pirate is gone,
Go down to your grog, boys, go down everyone.
Go down to your grog, boys, and be of good cheer.
The pirate has vanished so now have no fear.'

4. JESSE JAMES

Jesse James, the Robin Hood of the Wild West, was treacherously killed by Robert Ford, one of his own men, on 3 April 1882. Jesse was in hiding in St Joseph, Missouri, going under the name of 'Mr Howard'. He was not as noble a character as this song makes out.

2 It was Robert Ford, that dirty little coward.
  I wonder how that fella feels.
  For he ate of Jesse's bread, and he slept in Jesse's bed.
  And he laid poor Jesse in his grave.

3 It was on a Saturday night when Jesse was at home
  Talking with his family brave,
  Robert Ford came along like a thief in the night,
  And laid poor Jesse in his grave.

4 The people held their breath when they heard of Jesse's death,
  And wondered how he came to die.
  It was one of his own gang, called little Robert Ford,
  Had shot poor Jesse on the sly.

5 This song was made by Billy Gasshade
  As soon as the news did arrive,
  He said there was no man with the law in his hand
  Could take Jesse James when alive.

5. THE 'TITANIC'

The luxury liner *Titanic* went down with 1700 souls on the night of 14–15 April 1912, during her maiden voyage. So sure were the owners that she was unsinkable that there were insufficient lifeboats for the overcrowded ship.

10

2   Oh she was far from England
And approaching to the shore,
When the rich refused to associate with the poor.
So they put them down below
Where they were first to go.

3   As the humble closed their eyes
In the darkness of the hold,
The rich upstairs were playing cards for gold,
And they laughed when a sailor said,
'There's an iceberg close ahead.'

4   When the Captain heard the news
From a sailor up the mast,
He said, 'Steady boys, we'd better not go too fast.'
But the company in their greed
Said, 'We must increase the speed.'

5   Oh they put the lifeboats out,
O'er the raging stormy sea,
And the band on board played 'Nearer my God to Thee'.
Little children wept and cried
As the waves swept o'er the side.

6. CASEY JONES

John L. (Casey) Jones was an engine-driver who was always on time. On 30 April 1900 he was told to take over a train that was already eight hours late. He was determined to make up the lost time but a goods train protruding from a siding caused this fatal accident.

Come all you roun - ders— lis - ten here, I'll
tell you the sto - ry of a brave en - gi - neer.
Ca - sey Jones— was the hog - ger's name. On a
six - eight wheel - er, boys, he won his fame.
Cal - ler called Ca - sey at half - past four, he
kissed his wife— at the sta - tion door.
Moun - ted to the ca - bin with his or - ders in his hand and
took his fare - well trip— to the Pro - mised Land.
Ca - sey Jones moun - ted to the ca - bin. Ca - sey Jones with his

or - ders in his hand. Ca - sey Jones moun - ted to the ca - bin and took his fare - well trip____ to the Pro - mised Land.

last time

and took his fare - well trip ___ to the Pro - mised Land.

2 Put in your water and shovel in your coal,
Put your head out the window,
Watch the drivers roll.
'I'll run her till she leaves the rail
'Cause we're eight hours late with the Western Mail.'
He looked at his watch and his watch was slow,
Looked at the water and the water was low,
Turned to his fireboy, then he said,
'We're bound to reach 'Frisco
But we'll all be dead.'

3 Casey pulled up Reno Hill,
Tooted at the crossing
With an awful shrill.
'Snakes' all knew by the engine's moans
That the hogger at the throttle was Casey Jones.
He pulled up short two miles from the place,
Freight train stared him right in the face,
Turned to his fireboy, 'Son, you'd better jump
'Cause there's two locomotives
That are going to bump.'

4 Casey said just before he died
'There's two more roads
I'd like to ride.'
Fireboy asked, 'What can they be?'
'The Rio Grande and the Santa Fe.'
Mrs Jones sat on her bed a sigh'n,
Had a pink that her Casey was dy'n,
Said, 'Hush you children, stop your cry'n,
'Cause you'll get another Papa
On the Salt Lake Line.'

7. THE GRESFORD DISASTER

This tragedy occurred in 1934, apparently because dynamite charges were being used in a section of the pit that was heavy with gas.

You've heard of the Gres-ford dis - as - ter and the

ter - ri - ble price that was paid. Two

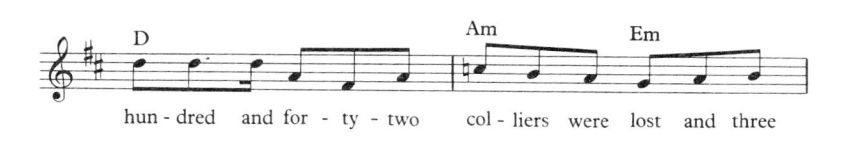

hun - dred and for - ty - two col - liers were lost and three

men of the res - cue bri - gade.

2 It occurred in the month of September,
At three in the morning, that pit
Was wracked by a violent explosion
In the 'Dennis' where gas lay so thick.

3 The gas in the 'Dennis' deep section
Was packed there like snow in a drift
And many a man had to leave the coal face
Before he had worked out his shift.

4 A fortnight before the explosion,
To the shot-firer, Tomlinson cried,
'If you fire that shot we'll be all blown to hell.'
And nobody can say that he lied.

5 The fireman's reports they are missing,
The records of forty-two days.
The colliery manager had them destroyed
To cover his criminal ways.

6 The Lord Mayor of London's collecting
To help both the children and wives.
The owners have sent some white lilies
To pay for the poor colliers' lives.

7 Down there in the dark they are lying,
They died for nine shillings a day,
They've worked out their shift, and it's now they must lie
In the darkness until Judgement Day.

8 Farewell all our wives and our children,
Farewell all our sweethearts as well.
Don't send your sons down the dark dreary mine,
They'll be damned like the sinners in hell.

8. ON A BRITISH SUBMARINE

Chief Petty Officer Tawney, R.N., made up this ballad. Cheering to order is a standing joke with 'matelots' and this incident pokes good fun at 'their Lordships' of the Admiralty.

It hap - pened on a sum - mer's day in

nine-teen fif - ty - four. We went to greet Her Ma - jes - ty a -

- com - in' from the Tour.* *On a Bri - tish sub - ma - rine, on a*

Bri -tish sub - ma - rine, when six - ty so - lid sai - lors were

cheer - in' of the Queen.

* South Africa.

2   Their Lordships said, 'Now cheer, my boys, and mind you make it smart.
There's nothing looks so ragged as cheering from the heart.'

3   But when we saw the signal, boys, it made our innards freeze.
'On the order "One" you hold your hats at forty-five degrees.'

4   At forty-five degrees, my boys, that's what their Lordships said,
'On the Order "Two" you wave your hats three times around your head.'

5   'And when you go to cheer, my boys, be careful what you say.
The word you use for cheering is "Hoora" and not "Hooray".'

6   We sailed towards *Britannia*, boys, the finest ever seen,
With every man a-standing like a petrified Marine.

7   But when we reached the moment, boys, that every skipper dreads,
A swarm of gnats as big as bats descended on our heads.

8   The boat was filled with waving arms and the air was filled with cries
As every matelot cursed and fought to keep 'em from his eyes.

9   The Duke he scratched his head as he watched us all depart.
'That's the first time I've seen sailor boys a-cheering from the heart!'

10   We waved our way across the bay till we were out of sight,
We waved our way all through the day and on into the night.

11   Ah, the day we met the Queen, my boys, that day I'll ne'er forget.
If we hadn't dived to ninety feet we'd all be waving yet!

Comic Songs

9. THE DERBY RAM

This story of a fabulous monster exists in many different versions. In Northumberland they have a similar song about the 'Lambton Worm'. There may be some connection between these songs and the hobby horse and other animals in May Day celebrations and Morris dances.

2 This ram was fat behind, sir,
   This ram was fat before.
   He measured ten yards round, sir,
   I think it was no more.

3 He had four feet to walk on, sir,
   He had four feet to stand,
   And every foot he had, sir,
   Did cover an acre of land.

4 The man who killed this ram, sir,
   Was drowned in all the blood,
   And he who held the dish, sir,
   Was carried away in the flood.

5 The mutton that ram made, sir,
   Gave all the Army meat,
   And what was left, I'm told, sir,
   Was served out to the Fleet.

6 The wool grew on his back, sir,
   It reached up to the sky,
   And there the eagles built their nests,
   I heard the young ones cry.

7 The wool grew on his belly, sir,
   It reached down to the ground,
   And that was sold in Derby town
   For forty thousand pound.

10. I ONCE WENT A-COURTING

The story of how the young couple get the better of their parents is as old as time and occurs in songs, stories, plays and operas all over the world.

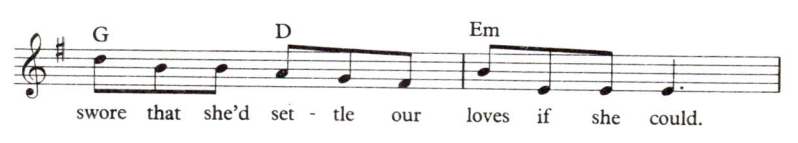

* Last time E major with G♯s in voice parts.

2   She shut to the window and bolted the door,
    Then I searched round the cottage behind and before,
    And when she popped t'door to, slap bang in my face,
    She thought I'd be off and abandon the chase.
                        (But I didn't)

3   She got an old farmer our wits for to puzzle,
    He loaded his blunderbuss up to the muzzle,
    And when he presented it close to my head,
    It went off with a bang and I thought I was dead.
                        (But I wasn't)

4   You may think now I didn't go many times more,
    Ever courting around this old woman's door.
    In singing this ditty, I haven't been long,
    You may think there's another long verse to my song.
                        (But there isn't)

11. THE FOX

An American version of a theme that also occurs in English folk-songs.

The fox went out one chil - ly night, prayed for the moon to give him light. He'd ma - ny a mile to go that night be - fore he reached the town O, town O, town O. He'd ma - ny a mile to go that night be - fore he reached the town O.

2 He ran till he came to a great big pen
   Where the geese and the ducks were laid therein.
   'A couple o'you gonna grease my chin
   Before I leave this town O.'

3 He grabbed the grey goose by the neck,
   Threw a duck across his back.
   He didn't mind their quack, quack, quack,
   And their legs all a-dangling down O.

4 Then Old Mother Flipper Flopper jumped out of bed,
   Out of the window she cocked her head,
   Crying, 'Hey John, the grey goose is gone,
   And the fox is on the town O.'

5 Then John he went to the top of the hill,
   And blew his horn both loud and shrill,
   Crying, 'Hey boys, better come for the kill,
   'Cause the fox is on the town O.'

6 He ran till he came to his cosy den.
   There were the little ones, eight, nine, ten,
   Saying, 'Hey, Dad, better go back again
   'Cause it must be a mighty fine town O.'

7 Then the fox and his wife without any strife
   Cut up the goose with a fork and a knife,
   They never had such a supper in their life,
   And the little ones chewed on the bones O.

12. OLD JOE CLARKE

This is a favourite American square dance tune and new verses are continually being made up to it. Joe Clarke was one of the pioneer settlers in Virginia.

2 Went down to Old Joe Clarke's house,
   He invited me to supper,
   Stubbed my toe on the table leg
   And stuck my nose in the butter.

3 Wish I had a sweetheart,
   I'd set her on a shelf,
   And every time she smiled at me
   I'd get up there myself.

4 I wouldn't marry an old maid.
   I'll tell you the reason why;
   Her neck's so long and stringy, boys,
   I'd fear she'd never die.

5 I wouldn't marry a widow,
   I'll tell you the reason why,
   She'd have so many children
   They'd make those biscuits fly.

6 I'll tell you who I'd marry,
   I'd marry Betsy Ann.
   'Cause Betsy Ann she ain't got much
   But she does the best she can.

13. OUT IN THE GREAT NORTHWEST

This song probably comes from the American music-halls of the 'Gold Rush' days.

I'm a go - in' way out West to where the buf - fa - lo used to roam. I'm goin' to try to set - tle down and build my - self a home. Out in the great North - west, way out in the great North - west. Men are men out there, I swear, they wres - tle with a griz - zly bear, punch his nose and comb his hair, way out in the great North - west.

2   I'll wear a big ten gallon hat and pack around a gun,
    I'll hunt ferocious bandits and I'll have a lot of fun.
        Out ....
    Men out there they have no fear, they rope a wild and woolly steer.
    Throw him down upon his ear, *way out* ....

3   There are so many fishes there in every mountain brook,
    You have to hide behind a tree to git to bait your hook.
        Out ....
    Rabbits there are very sly, they never go to school, but my, oh my,
    How those things can multiply, *way out* ....

4   A Scotsman he came there to live; he called his house a hoose,
    He saw a great big animal, they told him was a moose.
        Out ....
    The Scotsman he said 'What the deuce, you say you call this thing
        a moose?
    I'd hate to see a rat get loose,' *way out* ....

14. PRETTY POLLY PERKINS

One of the great favourites of the old music-hall, written and sung by one of its popular performers, Harry Clifton.

I'm a bro – ken heart-ed milk – man, in grief I'm ar – rayed, through keep – in' of the com – pa – ny of a young ser – vant maid who liv'd on board and wa – ges, the house to keep clean, in a gen – tle – man's fam – 'ly near Pad – ding – ton Green. She was bea – u – ti –ful as a but – ter-fly and as proud as a queen, was pret – ty lit – tle Pol – ly Per – kins of Pad – ding – ton Green.

2 Her eyes were as black as the pips of a pear,
  No rose in the garden with her cheeks could compare,
  Her hair hung in ringerlets so beautiful and long,
  I thought that she loved me, but I found I was wrong.

3 When I'd rattle in the morning and cry 'Milk below!',
  At the sound of my milkcans her face she would show,
  With a smile on her countenance and a laugh in her eye.
  If I thought she'd have loved me, I'd have lain down to die.

4 When I asked her to marry me, she said 'Oh, what stuff!'
  And told me to 'drop it' for she'd had quite enough
  Of my nonsense, at the same time I'd been very kind,
  But to marry a milkman she didn't feel inclined.

5 'Oh, the man that has me must have silver and gold,
  A chariot to ride in, and be handsome and bold.
  His hair must be curly as any watch spring,
  And his whiskers as big as a brush for clothing.'

6 The words that she uttered went straight thro' my heart,
  I sobbéd, I sighéd and straight did depart,
  With a tear on my eyelid as big as a bean,
  With a goodbye to Polly of Paddington Green.

7 In six months she married, this hard-hearted girl,
  But it was not a Viscount and it was not a Nearl.
  It was not a Baronet but a shade or two wuss,
  'Twas a bowlegged Conductor of a Company Bus.

15. MRS McGRATH

This is an Irish street ballad. There are still street-singers and wandering fiddle-players in Ireland who make up their own music day by day. There is often an odd sense of humour in Irish songs. Here, for instance it is very difficult to take Ted's plight as seriously as we ought.

2   Now Mrs McGrath lived on the seashore
For the space of seven long years or more
Till she saw a big ship sailing in the bay,
'Hullaloo, bullaloo, and I think it's he!'

3   'O Captain dear where have you been?
Have you been sailing on the Mediterreen?
And have you any tidings of my son Ted?
Is the poor boy living or is he dead?'

4   Then up comes Ted without any legs
And in their place two wooden pegs.
She kissed him a dozen times or two,
Saying, 'Holy Moses, it isn't you!'

5   'O were you drunk or were you blind
That you left your two fine legs behind?
Or was it walking upon the sea
Wore your two fine legs from your knees away?'

6   'O, I wasn't drunk and I was'nt blind,
But I left my two fine legs behind,
For a cannonball on the fifth of May
Took my two fine legs from my knees away.'

7   'O Teddy, me boy,' the widow cried,
'Your two fine legs were your mama's pride.
Them stumps of a tree won't do at all.
Why didn't you run from the big cannonball?'

16. MRS HOOLIGAN'S CHRISTMAS CAKE

Another Irish street-song, which probably started in the music-halls.

As I sat in me win-dow last eve-nin'___ a
There were plums and prunes and cher-ries,___

let-ter-man came un-to me___ He had a
rais-ins and cur-rants and cin-na-mon too. There were

nice lit-tle neat in-vi-ta-tion,___ say-ing
nuts and cloves and ber-ries___ but the

'Won't you come o-ver to tea?'___ I
crust it was nailed on with glue.___ There were

knew it was Hoo-li-gan sent it___ so I
ca-ra-way seeds in a-bun-dance,___ 'twould

went for our friend-ship's sake,___ and the
give you a fine head-ache,___ 'Twould kill

first thing he gave me to tack-le___ was a

32

slice of Mrs Hoo - li - gan's cake.

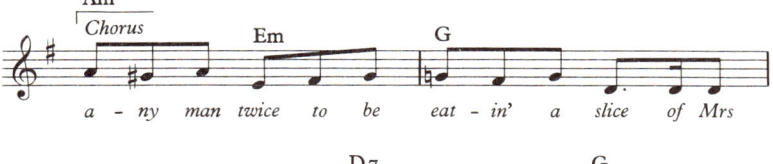

a - ny man twice to be eat - in' a slice of Mrs

Hoo - li - gan's Christ - mas cake.

2 Miss Mulligan wanted to taste it,
But really it was all no use.
She worked at it for over an hour
But couldn't get any of it loose.
Till Hooligan went for the hatchet,
And Kelly came in with the saw.
That cake was enough, by the power,
To paralyse any man's jaw.

Small notes refer to chorus *melody.*

Love Songs

17. THE GOLDEN WHEAT

Wales has given us some beautiful songs, and many people think this is the most beautiful of them all. (English words by Will Sanhow.)

2 O tell me truly, gentle Ann, O truly give your answer.
   Will you be mine for evermore or do you love another?
   Until the salt dries in the sea and whilst my eyes can seek you,
   Until my heart dies in my breast, I'll surely, surely, love you.

18. A LA CLAIRE FONTAINE

French Canadian in origin, this is a favourite with young and old in both communities and is sung wherever French-speaking people are gathered together.

2 Chante, rossignol, chante.
  Toi qui as le cœur gai.
  Tu as le cœur à rire,
  Moi je l'ai-t-à pleurer.

3 C'est pour mon ami Pierre
  Qui ne veut plus m'aimer
  Pour un bouton de rose
  Que lui ai refusé.

4 Je voudrais que la rose
  Fût encore au rosier
  Et que mon ami Pierre
  Fût encore à m'aimer.

1 Cool water, cool spring water,
  Shade of the chestnut tree,
  Just like my jealous lover,
  Cold as yon spring to me.
    Ever and ever I love him
    Yet he will ne'er love me.

2 Sweet nightingale up yonder,
  Your song is not for me,
  You sing of joy and laughter,
  I sing of misery.

3 He begged a rose I'd gathered,
  But I would not agree.
  Now how I wish that rose
  Were back on the briar tree.

tr. G.B.

19. SLEIGH SONG

A cheerful love-song from the Soviet Union. All the winter the snow is many feet deep and frozen hard. In former times transport over the wilder areas was by horse-drawn sleigh, which skimmed over the top of the snow, drawn usually by three horses. Such a sleigh was called a *troika*.

O'er the snow my sleigh goes speed - ing, un - der -
Loud we hear the har - ness jin - gle, and the

- neath the fros - ty sky. And the hor - ses
dri - ver sings a song. Eyes a - flame and

need no lead - ing, thro' the night to my love they fly.
cheeks a - tin - gle, mer - ri - ly __ we __ race a - long.

Trot - ting, trot - ting, trot - ting, __ ne - ver stop - ping, __
Sing - ing, sing - ing, sing - ing, __ sleigh - bells ring - ing, __

through the night __ to my love they fly.
mer - ri - ly __ we __ race a - long.

tr. G.B.

20. THE RED RIVER VALLEY

Originally an American popular song of the nineteenth century called 'In the bright Mohawk Valley', this tune was taken over by cowboys and became their favourite love-song.

2 When you go to your home o'er the ocean,
   O remember the many happy hours
   That you spent in the Red River Valley,
   And the love we exchanged midst its bowers.

3 And should you ever return
   To this lone prairie land of the West,
   May the white girl you marry remember
   That the red maiden loved you the best.

21. BALLINDERRY

A song from Northern Ireland. The accompanying part is traditional.

It's plea-sant to be in Bal – lin-der-ry, it's pret-ty to be in Au -chal-lee. It's pret-tier to be___ in bon-ny Ram's Is - land, sit-ting un-der an i - vy tree.

2
O that I were in bon-ny Ram's Is - land.

O that I were with Phe-lin my dia - mond. She would whis-tle and I would sing and we would make the whole is - land ring.

Drone accompaniment:
(any octave)

och - one, och - one,

Repeat first verse and hum the tune once, dying away to finish. The 'drone' keeps going throughout the whole song.

22. NELLIE GRAY

An American popular ballad of the nineteenth century based on the true story of a white American soldier whose Negro bride was taken from him, back into slavery.

There's a low green val-ley by the old Kentuck-y shore, where I've whil'd ma-ny hap-py hours a - way, a - sit - tin' and a-sing-in' by the lit - tle cot-tage door, where dwelt my_ love-ly Nel-lie Gray. *O my poor Nel-lie Gray, they have ta - ken her a - way and I'll ne - ver see my dar-lin' an - y more. I am sit - tin' by the ri - ver and I'm weep - in' all the day for you've gone from the old Ken-tuck-y shore.*

2 One night I went to see her
But 'She's gone' the neighbours say.
The white man bound her with his chain.
They have taken her to Georgia
For to wear her life away,
As she toils in the cotton and the cane.

3 My eyes are getting blinded
And I cannot see the way.
Hark, there's somebody knocking at my door!
Oh, I hear the angels singing,
And I see my Nellie Gray!
Farewell to the old Kentucky shore.

✝ 23. THE FIREMAN'S NOT FOR ME

A twentieth-century folk-song by the Scots singer and writer, Ewan MacColl.

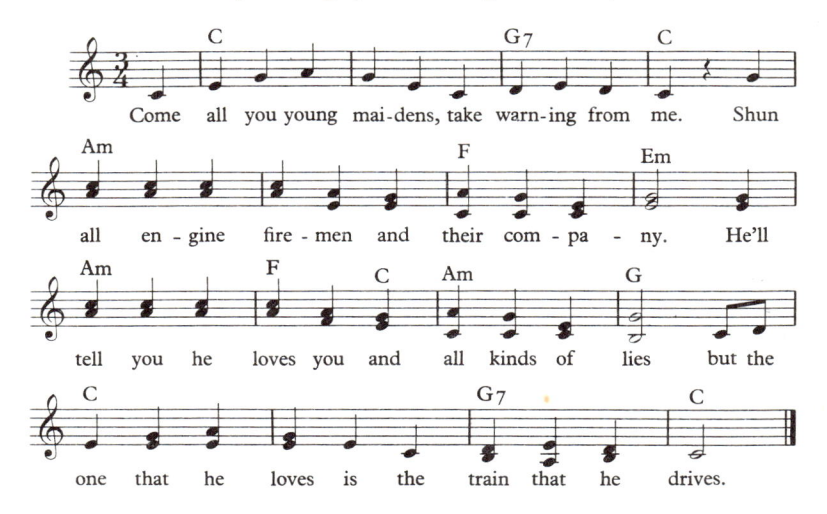

Come all you young mai-dens, take warn-ing from me. Shun all en – gine fire - men and their com - pa – ny. He'll tell you he loves you and all kinds of lies but the one that he loves is the train that he drives.

2 I once loved a fireman and he said he loved me,
He took me a-walking into the country.
He hugged me and kissed me and gazed in my eyes
And said, 'You're as nice as the eight forty-five.'

3 He said 'My dear Molly, O will you be mine?
Just give me the signal and let's clear the line.
My fires they are burning, my steam it is high,
If you don't take the brakes off I fear I shall die.'

4 I gave him this answer saying, 'Don't make so free,
For no engine fireman shall ever have me.
He says that he loves you then when you're in need,
He races away at the top of his speed.

5 A sailor comes home when his voyage is done.
A soldier gets weary of following the drum.
A collier will stick to his sweetheart for life,
But a fireman's one love is the engine—his wife.'

Songs of Affection

24. COSSACK LULLABY

The Cossacks of Southern Russia have long been famous as great horsemen and warriors. In the days of tribal warfare the men were away from home for long periods, and young boys were taken off to fight as soon as they were old enough.

Rest your head, my babe, my dar - ling.
Lul - la, lul - la - by.
Round your bed the shades are fal - ling.
Lul - la, lul - la - by.

2 Far away your valiant father fights and breaks my heart.
   Sleep, my baby, gently slumber. Some day, we, too, must part.

Repeat verse 1.

tr. G.B.

25. OLD PAINT

A cowboy's love-song to his horse. 'Paint' comes from the Spanish for horse—
pinto.

2 Old Biff Jones had two daughters and a song,
   One went to Denver, the other went wrong.
   His wife she died in a poolroom fight,
   But still he keeps singin' from mornin' to night.

3 When I die take my saddle from the wall,
   Lead out my pony, lead him out of his stall,
   Tie my bones to the saddle, turn his face towards the West,
   And we'll ride the prairie that we love the best.

* Descant to 'ah' or 'mm'.

26. SANDGATE DANDLING SONG

These tender words were written in the early nineteenth century by a blind fiddler called Robert Nunn, who played in the Tyneside pubs on pit pay-nights.

*A - oo - a my bon - ny bairn.   A - oo - a up - on my airm.

A - oo - a, ye soon may learn to   say 'Da - da' se can - ny. I

wish tha Dad - dy may be weel, he's lang a - com - in' from the keel. Tho'

his black face is like the de'il, I   like a kiss from John - ny.

2 Tha canny dowp is fat and round, and like tha dad, thou's plump and sound.
Thou's worth to me ten thousand pound, thou's altogether bonny.
When daddy's drunk he'll take a knife, and threaten sore to take my life.
Who wouldn't be a keelman's wife, to have a man like Johnny?

3 But yonder daddy's coming now, he looks the best among the crew.
They're all gan' to the 'Barley Mow'—my canny, godlike Johnny.
Come let's get the bacon fried and let us make a clean fireside,
Then on his knee he will thee ride, when he comes home to mammy.

4 A-oo-a, my bonny bairn. A-oo-a upon my airm.
A-oo-a, ye soon may learn to say 'Dada' se canny.
I wish tha Daddy may be weel, he's lang a-comin' from the keel.
Tho' his black face is like the de'il, I like a kiss from Johnny.

* Small notes to 'la'.

27. MY GRANDFATHER'S CLOCK

Written in 1876 by Henry Clay Work—an American popular songwriter who was also responsible for 'Marching through Georgia'.

2   In watching its pendulum swing to and fro
    Many hours had he spent while a boy.
    And in childhood and manhood the clock seemed to know,
    And to share both his trouble and his joy.
    For it struck twenty-four when he opened up the door
    With a blooming and beautiful bride,
    But it stopped short, never to go again, when the old man died.

3   My grandfather said that of those he could hire
    Not a servant so faithful he found,
    For it wasted no time and had but one desire
    At the end of each week to be wound.
    And it kept in its place, not a frown upon its face,
    And its hands never hung by its side,
    But it stopped short, never to go again, when the old man died.

28. WEGGIS

Weggis is on the shores of Lake Lucerne in Switzerland.

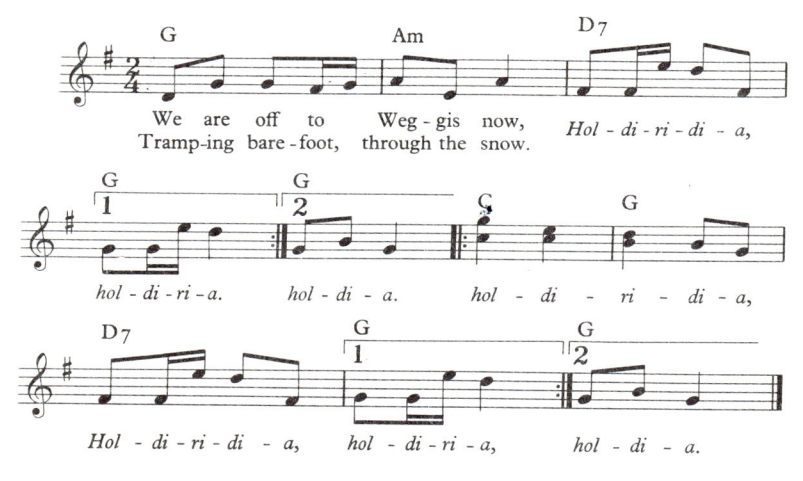

We are off to Weg-gis now,
Tramp-ing bare-foot, through the snow. *Hol - di - ri - di - a,*

hol - di - ri - a. *hol - di - a.* *hol - di - ri - di - a,*

Hol - di - ri - di - a, hol - di - ri - a, hol - di - a.

2 On the shore of Lake Lucerne,
We shall watch the fishes turn.

3 On the mountain peak so far,
Shout to heaven 'Heisasa!'

tr. G.B.

29. JAMAICA FAREWELL

A song by 'Lord' Burgess, one of the West Indies' leading calypso writers.

Down a - way where the nights are gay and the

sun shines dai - ly on the moun – tain top, ____ I took a trip on a sail - in' ship and when I reached Ja-mai - ca I made a stop. *But I'm sad to say, __ I'm on my way, __ won't be back __ for ma-ny a day. __ Me heart is down, me head is turn - in' a - round. I had to leave a lit - tle girl in King - ston town. __*

2 Down by the market you can hear
Lady cry out while on their heads they bear
'Ackee',* rice, or fish on ice,
And the rum is fine any time of year.

3 Sounds of laughter everywhere
And the dancing girls sway to and fro.
I must declare that my heart is there,
Though I've been from Maine to Mexico.

* Vegetables.

30. UN CANADIEN ERRANT

A 'homesick' song from Canada of the loneliness of a soldier captured far from home.

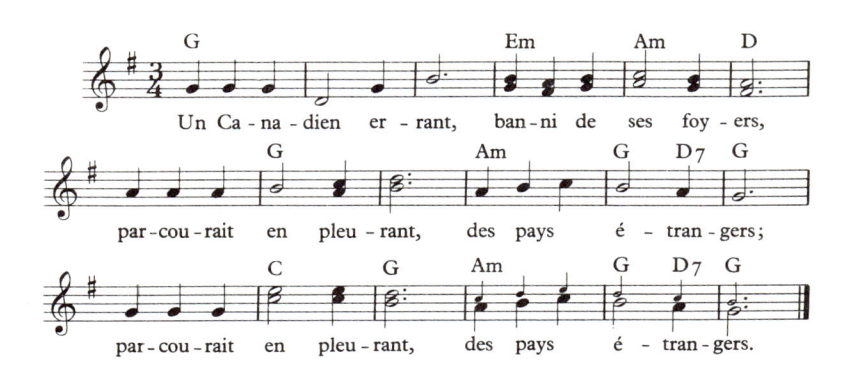

2 Un jour, triste et pensif, assis au bord des flots,
  Au courant fugitif, il adressa ces mots.

3 'Si tu vois mon pays, mon pays malheureux,
  Va dire à mes amis que je me souviens d'eux.

4 'O jours si pleins d'appas vous êtes disparus,
  Et ma patrie, hélas, je ne la verrai plus.

5 'Non, mais en expirant, O mon cher Canada,
  Mon regard languissant vers toi se portera.'

       ★   ★   ★

1 Lonely and far away, captive in distant wars,
  Roam'd a Canadian boy far from his native shores.

2 Wandering on, one day down by the ocean's side,
  This poor Canadian boy turned to the waves and cried,

3 'If you should ever see the land that to me is home,
  Tell all my friends from me I shall remember them.

4 'If in these lands I die, Canada weep for me,
  As in my dying hour, my eyes are turned to thee.'

31. DIRTY OLD TOWN

Another twentieth-century folk-song by Ewan MacColl.

2 I heard a siren from the dock,
   Saw a train set the night on fire,
   Smelt the Spring on a smoky wind.

3 We're going to make a good sharp axe,
   Shining steel, tempered in the fire,
   We'll chop you down like an old dead tree.

32. LEAVE HER JOHNNY

Sung by seamen in the days of sail, as they came home to port after a long voyage.

O ___ times are hard and ___ wa - ges are low.
Leave her John - ny leave her. O ___ times are ___ hard and ___
wa - ges are low. It's time for us to leave her.

2 The rain it rains the whole day long,
   The North-east wind is blowing strong.

3 Mahogany beef and weevilled bread,
   We wish old Leatherface was dead.

4 I thought I heard our captain say,
   'Tomorrow you will get your pay.'

Repeat verse 1 to finish.

Songs of Work and Drink

33. FOURPENCE A DAY

A song from the dark days of the nineteenth century, when little children were made to work long hours for a miserable wage. This boy works washing the ore in the Yorkshire lead mines. Verse 2 tells of the 'knockers-up' who woke all the workers so that they got to the factory on time. If you were late you were shut out and lost the day's wages.

The ore's a-wait-in' in the tubs, the snow's up-on the fell.____ Can-ny folk are sleep-in' yet but lead is reet to sell. ____ Come my lit-tle wash-er lad—,__ come,__ let's a-way. __ We're bound down to sla-ve-ry for four-pence a day.____

2 It's early in the morning, we rise at five o'clock
And the little slaves come to the door to knock, knock, knock.
Come my little washer lad, come, let's away,
It's very hard to work for fourpence a day.

3 My father was a miner, he lived down in the town,
'Twas hard work and poverty that always kept him down.
He aimed for us to go to school, but brass he couldn't pay,
So we had to go to the washing rake for fourpence a day.

4 Fourpence a day, my lad, and very hard to work,
And never a pleasant word from a gruffy lookin' 'Turk'.*
His conscience it may fail and his heart it may give way,
Then he'll raise us our wages to ninepence a day.

* Foreman.

34. LES TISSERANDS

A French song about the weavers, who never seem to get down to any work.

Les tis - ser - ands sont

pire que les é - vê - ques. Tous les lun - dis, ils

s'en font - u - ne fê - te. *Et tipe et tape et tipe et tape, est -*

- il trop gros, est - il trop fin, et cou - cher tard le - ver ma - tin.

En rou - lant la na - vet - te le beau temps vien - dra.

2 Tous les lundis, ils s'en font une fête
Et les mardis, ils ont mal à la tête.

3 Tous les mardis, ils ont mal à la tête,
Le mercredi, ils vont charger leur pièce,

4 Le mercredi, ils vont charger leur pièce,
Et le jeudi, ils vont voir leur maîtresse.

5 Et le jeudi, ils vont voir leur maîtresse,
Le vendredi, ils travaillent sans cesse.

6 Le vendredi, ils travaillent sans cesse,
Le samedi, la pièce n'est pas faite,

7 Le samedi, la pièce n'est pas faite,
Et le dimanche, il faut de l'argent maître.

★   ★   ★

1 Those weaving men are worse than any bishop fine.
On Monday morn they stay in bed till dinnertime.
And tick and tack and tick and tack, the shuttles go and
*   then come back, but goodness how those weavers slack!*
Just give us one more hour and then perhaps we'll come.

2 On Monday morn, they stay in bed till dinnertime,
On Tuesday, they just laugh and eat and drink their wine.

3 On Tuesday, they just laugh and eat and drink their wine,
On Wednesday, they decide they'll start to work at nine.

4 On Wednesday, they decide they'll start to work at nine,
On Thursday, oh, so tired, they sleep all day again.

5 On Thursday, oh, so tired they sleep all day again,
On Friday, well, they work if it's wet but don't if it's fine.

6 On Friday, well, they work if it's wet but don't if it's fine,
On Saturday, it's too late to do the job in time.

7 On Saturday, it's too late to do the job in time,
When Sunday comes they find they haven't earned a dime.

tr. G.B.

35. I'VE BEEN WORKING ON THE RAILROAD

This is a very popular American college song which may have started as a traditional working song. The last part is just nonsense and has been added to the original tune by students. The first line is slow. The rest, after the pause, is fairly fast.

Di - nah won't you blow, Di - nah won't you blow,

Di - nah won't you blow your horn?_____ horn?

Some - one's in the kitch - en with Di - nah,

some - one's in the kitch - en I know._____

Some - one's in the kitch - en with Di - nah,

strum - min' on the old ban - jo. Fee, fi,

fid - dly - i - o, fee, fi, fid - dly - i - o,_____

fee, fi, fid - dly - i - o, strum - min' on the old ban - jo.

36. THE HOUSEWIFE'S LAMENT

This song was found in the diary of a lady in Illinois, who lived at the time of the American Civil War.

One day I was walk-ing, I heard a com-plain-ing and saw an old wo-man the pic-ture of gloom. She gazed at the mud on her door-step, 'twas rain-ing, and this was her song as she wield-ed her broom. *O life is a toil and love is a trou-ble. Beau-ty will fade and rich-es will flee. Plea-sures they dwin-dle and pri-ces they dou-ble and no-thing is as I would wish it to be.*

2   There's too much of worriment goes to a bonnet,
There's too much of ironing goes to a shirt,
There's nothing that pays for the time you waste on it,
There's nothing that lasts but trouble and dirt.

3   In March it is mud, it is slush in December,
The mid-summer breezes·are loaded with dust.
In fall the leaves litter, in muddy September
The wallpaper rots and the candlesticks rust.

4   It's sweeping at six and it's dusting at seven.
It's victuals at eight and it's dishes at nine.
It's potting and panning from ten to eleven.
We've scarce finished breakfast, we're ready to dine.

5   Last night in my dreams I was stationed forever
On a far little rock in the midst of the sea.
My one chance of life was a ceaseless endeavour.
To sweep off the waves as they swept over me.

6   Alas! 'Twas no dream; ahead I behold it,
I see I am helpless my fate to avert.
She lay down her broom, her apron she folded,
She lay down and died, and was buried in dirt.

37. WHALING IN GREENLAND

This was a most dangerous kind of fishing. Boats were lowered and the whale was tackled at close quarters, and it could easily capsize the craft with a flick of its tail.

They signed us wea - ry wha - ler - men for the i - cy Green-land ground. They said we'd take a score of __ whale while we was out-ward bound, *brave boys*, while ___ we was out - ward bound.

2. The lookout up in the barrel stood, a spyglass in his hand.
   'There's a whale, there's a whale, there's a whalefish!' he cried,
   'And she blows at every span.'

3. The captain stood on the quarter deck, the ice was in his eye.
   'Overhaul, overhaul, let your davit*-tackles fall,
   And put your boats to sea.'

4. The harpoon struck, the line ran out, the whale gave a flurry with his tail,
   And he upset the boat, we lost half a dozen men,
   And we never caught that whale.

5. 'Bad news, bad news', our captain said, and it grieved his heart full sore,
   But the losing of a hundred-barrel† whale,
   Oh, it grieved him ten times more.

6. The winter star did then appear, it was time to anchor weigh,
   To stow below our running gear,
   And homeward bear away.

7. Oh! Greenland is an awful place, a land that's never green,
   Where there's ice and snow and the whalefish blow,
   And the daylight's seldom seen.

* Pronounce 'day-vit'.
† A whale that produced a hundred barrels of oil. According to A. L. Lloyd, this would be an impossible catch anyway.

38. THE CALTON WEAVER

Calton is a part of Glasgow, and weaving was an important trade there in the old days. Weavers would hawk their wares about and gather in the evenings to drink and sing. Whisky, here, is compared with a girl who gets you in her clutches and never lets you go.

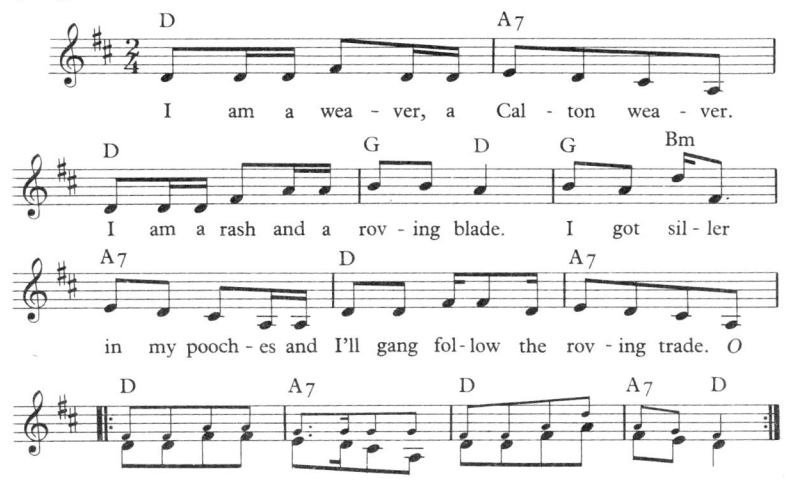

Whis-ky, Whis-ky, Nan-cy Whis-ky. Whis-ky, Whis-ky Nan-cy O.

2 As I came in by Glesga city
Nancy Whisky I chanced to smell.
I went in and sat beside her,
Seven long years I loved her well.

3 The more I kissed her the more I loved her,
The more I kissed her the more she smiled,
Till I forgot my mother's teaching;
Nancy soon had me beguiled.

4 I woke early in the morning,
To slake my throat it was my need:
I tried to rise but I was not able,
For Nancy had me by the head.

5 Come all you weavers, Calton weavers,
Come all you weavers, where e'er you be.
Beware of Whisky, Nancy Whisky,
She'll ruin you as she ruined me.

39. CHEVALIERS DE LA TABLE RONDE

France's most popular drinking-song—the drink being, of course, wine in this case.

2 J'en boirai cinq ou six bouteilles,
   Une femme sur mes genoux.

3 Toc, Toc, Toc, on frappe à la porte,
   Je crois bien que c'est le mari.

4 Si c'est lui, que le diable l'emporte,
   De venir troubler mon plaisir.

5 Si je meurs, je veux qu'on m'enterre
   Dans une cave où'l y a du bon vin.

6 Les deux pieds contre la muraille,
   Et la tête sous le robinet.

7 La morale de cette histoire
   C'est de boire avant de mourir.

1 Friends of mine, friends all met together,
  Taste the wine, tell me if it's good.
    Taste the wine, *oui, oui, oui*,⋆
    Taste the wine, *non, non, non*,⋆
    Taste the wine, tell me if it's good.

2 Put me down for a dozen bottles,
  Tell my girl to come and sit with me.

3 Knock, knock, knock, that must be her husband,
  Might have known he'd be after me.

4 If it's him, tell him he's a spoilsport,
  Coming here when I'm having fun.

5 If he gets me, let me be buried
  Underground in a cellar cool.

6 My two feet propped against a barrel
  And my head underneath a bung.

7 There's a moral to this story,
  Drink your wine down before you die.

⋆ 'Oui, oui, oui', 'non, non, non', is best retained even in the English version, but put in 'yes' and 'no' if you prefer.

tr. **G.B.**

40. FILL HER UP!

The Russians do nothing by halves—and drinking is no exception. Your glass of vodka must go down in one gulp, and there will be many gulps in an evening! This Russian student song is very slow and 'beery' up to the double bar, but the last part is very fast.

2 My mother would scold me if she could see me now, boys
   For she's often told me I keep bad company.

tr. G.B.

41. FINE GIRL YOU ARE!

You don't have to sing the chorus of this one; you shout it. This is the Irish version of a fine old song known as 'Swansea Town'. The 'holy ground' is Ireland.

Fare thee well my love - ly Di - nah, a thou-sand times fare - well, for I am going to leave you now, the truth to you I'll tell and the se - crets of my mind. *Fine girl you are!* You're the girl that I a - dore; and now I live in hope to see the ho - ly ground once more. *Fine girl you are!*

2 And now the storm is raging
And we are far from cove,
And the poor old ship she's sinking fast
And her riggings they are tore,
And the secrets of my mind
Fine girl you are!
You're the girl that we adore,
And still we live in hope to see,
The holy ground once more.
Fine girl you are!

3 And now the storm is over,
  And we are safe in cove,
  And we'll drink one toast to the holy ground
  And the girl that we adore.
  And we'll drink strong ale and porter
  Fine girl you are!
  And we'll make the taproom roar,
  And when our money is all spent
  We'll go to sea once more.
  Fine girl you are!

Songs from the Stage

42. MAN, MAN, MAN
(*The Mock Marriage*—1696)

Henry Purcell lived in the days of Charles II, Samuel Pepys and the Great Fire of London. Theatre-going was very popular then and Purcell was employed to write songs, like this one, to be sung in the course of plays. He also wrote plays which were nearly all songs and music—like the musical shows of today.

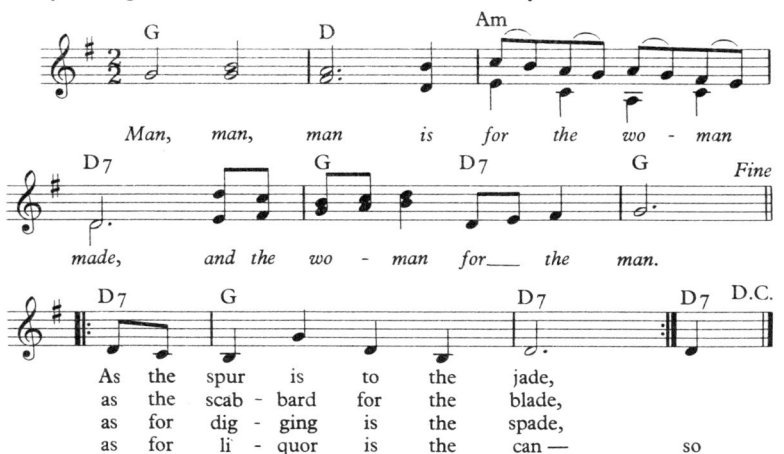

Man, man, man is for the wo - man made, and the wo - man for____ the man.

As the spur is to the jade,
as the scab - bard for the blade,
as for dig - ging is the spade,
as for li - quor is the can —   so

2 As the sceptre to be sway'd, as for nights the serenade,
  As for pudding is the pan, and to cool us is the fan—

3 Be she widow, be she maid, be she wanton, be she staid,
  Be she well or ill array'd, queen, slut or harridan--

43. THE WATERMAN
(The Waterman—1774)

This song is from a little musical play called *The Waterman*, by Charles Dibdin, who was a very popular singer and songwriter in the days of Admiral Nelson. Dibdin was one of the first musicians to make a fortune out of light, popular songs and shows.

And did you not hear of a jol-ly young wa-ter-man who at Black-fri-ars Bridge used for to ply? And he feather-ed his oars with such skill and dex-ter-i-ty, win-ning each heart and de-light-ing each eye. He looked so neat and rowed so stead-i-ly, the maid-ens all flocked to his boat so read-i-ly. And he eyed the young rogues with so

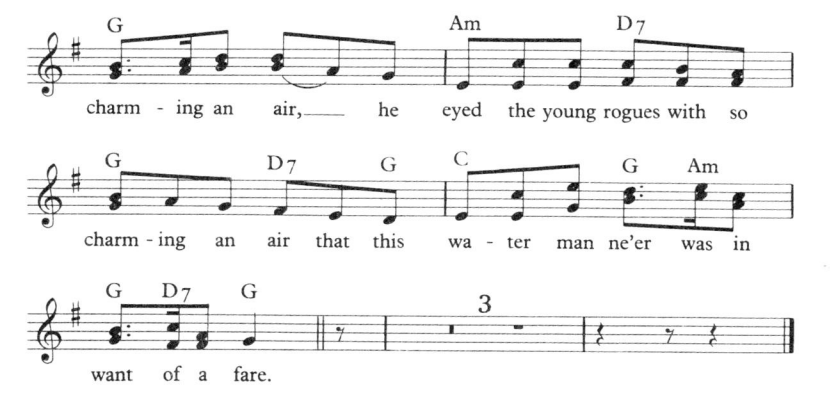

charm - ing an air,__ he eyed the young rogues with so

charm - ing an air that this wa - ter man ne'er was in

want of a fare.

2 What sights of fine folks he oft rowed in his wherry,
   'Twas cleaned out so nice and so painted withal.
   He was always 'first oars' when the fine city ladies
   In a party to Ranelagh★ went, or Vauxhall.★
   And oft times would they be giggling or leering,
   But 'twas all one to Tom, their gibing and jeering:
   For loving and liking he little did care, (*twice*)
   For this waterman ne'er was in want of a fare.

3 And yet but to see how strangely things happen.
   As he row'd along, thinking of nothing at all,
   He was ply'd by a damsel so lovely and charming,
   And she smiled and so straightway in love did he fall:
   And would this young damsel but banish his sorrow
   He'd wed her tonight, before e'en tomorrow:
   And how should this waterman ever know care, (*twice*)
   When he's married and ne'er in want of a fare.

★ Pleasure gardens.

67

44. SAY GOODBYE NOW
(The Marriage of Figaro—1786)

Many people think Mozart wrote the best comic operas in the theatre. It is a pity more people did not think so during his lifetime or he might have had a more successful career. Only *Don Giovanni* and *The Marriage of Figaro* had any success and he died, at 35, with hardly a penny to his name. This is probably the most well-known tune he ever wrote, and caught on like wildfire whenever the opera was performed.

Say good-bye now to pas-time and play, lad. Say good-bye to your airs and your gra - ces. Here's an end to the life that was gay, lad. Here's an end to your games with the girls. Here's an end to the life that was gay, lad. Here's an end to your games with the girls.

Not for you now are rib-bons and la - ces.

Not for you frills and feath-ers and fa - vours. Pink and

white like a girl's tho' your face is, you must

lose all your ring - lets and curls. You must

lose all your ring - lets and curls. Not for

you are frills and feathers, curls and ring-lets, airs and

gra - ces and sweet pret - ty fa - ces. *Say good-*

- bye now to pas - time and play, lad. Say good-

- bye to your airs and your gra - ces. Here's an

end to the life that was gay, lad. Here's an

end to your games with the girls. Here's an

end to the life that was gay, lad. Here's an

end to your games with the girls.

Chest thrown out and should-ers back, sir!

Hold your head up, not so slack, sir! Take your

musk - et on your should - er, that's the right style for a

sold - ier. Du-ty calls you to death or glo - ry. As to

pay, that's an - o - ther sto - ry, quite an - o - ther

sto - ry, quite an - o - ther sto - ry. No more

dan - ces now but train - ing for the plea - sures of cam -

- paign -ing. Yes, you'll find it quite ex - ci-ting,

when you come to do some fight-ing, bu - gles cal - ling, sa - bres

flash-ing, can -nons roar-ing, mor -tars crash-ing, head-long in - to dan - ger

dash - ing, that's the life you've got in store. Not for

you are frills and feathers. Not for you curls and

ringlets. Not for you airs and gra-ces. Not for

you are sweet pret - ty fa - ces. *Say good*

bye now to pas - time and play, lad. Say good

bye to your airs and your gra - ces. Here's an

end to the life that was gay, lad. Here's an

end to your games with the girls. Here's an

end to the life that was gay, lad. Here's an

end to your games with the girls. Some day you'll come back vic -

- to -rious, if you don't get killed be - fore! Then you'll

swear that war is glo -rious. Oh, a glo - rious thing is

war. Oh, a glo - rious thing is war. Oh, a

glo - rious thing is war.

45. HUNTSMEN'S CHORUS

(*Der Freischütz*—1821)

Weber was a German who wrote some very popular grand operas in Regency times. He liked horrific subjects with ghosts, witches, ruined castles and moonlight forests. This chorus is from *Der Freischütz* (*The Marksman*), a story of hunting, shooting matches and magic bullets.

2 Refreshed from our sleep, in the cool morning riding,
   The wolf and the boar in the wood best beware.
   We'll be on their track when they come out of hiding,
   And then we'll give chase and get rid of the pair.

* Some voices can sing this bar throughout the chorus.

tr. G.B.

46. BRINDISI
(*La Traviata*—1853)

La Traviata is a tragic opera by an Italian, Giuseppe Verdi, but near the opening is this cheerful drinking chorus.

Let's laugh___ and be hap - py while life is still ours ___ to sing and__ to __ dance and __ make. mer - ry in. There's no ___ earth - ly rea - son for wor - ry, so laugh___ and chase sor - row_ and _ care far__ a - way. A health to you fair___ la - dies here and may you ne - ver___ leave us, for it would sore - ly___ grieve us to see you

on your_____ way_____ We'll laugh_____ and we'll sing and we'll dance all this eve - - ning, this eve - ning, this _ night and_ next_ day, all_____ this eve - ning, this_ night and_ next_ day. day._____

2   There's no sense in spending your time in complaining,
There's time for all that when you're older.
In youth, there's no point in your ever abstaining
From pleasures that may fade away.
A flower may grow and die one hour,
Unknown and unadmired.
So let us be inspired
To take what pleasure we may.

tr. G.B.

47. THE BOLD GENDARMES

(Geneviève de Brabant—1875)

Jacques Offenbach, the Frenchman who wrote this song, was the man who gave Gilbert and Sullivan the idea of writing comic operas. His own were enjoying a huge success in Paris at that time.

2   Sometimes our duty's extra-mural, then little butterflies we chase.
We like to gambol in things rural. Commune with nature face to face.
Unto our beat then back returning, refreshed by nature's holy charm,

3   If gentlemen will make a riot, and punch each other's heads at night,
We're quite disposed to keep it quiet, provided that they make it right!
But if they do not seem to see it or give us our proper terms,

48. GYPSIES' CHORUS

*(Carmen—*1875)

Carmen is one of the most exciting and colourful of operas. It is by a Frenchman—Georges Bizet—but it is set in Spain. Carmen is a very attractive but very wild girl who captivates a simple soldier, Don José. In this chorus she is dancing and singing with her gypsy friends.

The gyp-sies love to sing and dance. When-ev-er they hear mu-sic play - ing, they'll tap their feet and start a - sway - ing. Those gyp-sies love to sing and dance. The tam-bour-ines and cym-bals ring and as the sound be-gins to swell, — the soft gui-tars be-gin to sing to that re - frain they know so well, to that re -

* Small notes for last verse.

2   And in the blinking firelight glow,
Their rings and bangles brightly gleaming,
Their skirts and flounces round them spinning,
Those dusky girls sway to and fro.
The tapping feet begin to stamp,
And now the men take up their stance,
From every corner of the camp
The gypsies come to join the dance. *(twice)*

3   And now the dance is at its height,
And faster now the music's playing,
And faster now the dancers swaying,
Their voices echo through the night.
And to that tapping, tapping beat,
They all surrender in a trance,
And with their stamping, stamping feet,
Keep up the frenzy of the dance. *(twice)*

1   Les tringles des sistres tintaient
Avec un éclat métallique,
Et sur cette étrange musique
Les Zingarelles se levaient.
Tambours de Basque allaient leur train
Et les guitares forcenées
Grinçaient sous les mains obstinées,
Même chanson, même refrain. *(twice)*

2   Les anneaux de cuivre et d'argent
Reluisaient sur les peaux bistrées.
D'orange et de rouge zébrées,
Les étoffes flottaient au vent.
La danse au chant se mariait,
La danse au chant se mariait.
D'abord indécise et timide,
Plus vive ensuite et plus rapide,
Cela montait, montait, montait, montait.

3   Les Bohémiens à tour de bras
De leurs instruments faisaient rage,
Et cet éblouissant tapage
Ensorcelait les Zingaras.
Sous le rythme de la chanson,
Sous le rythme de la chanson.
Ardentes, folles et enfièvrées,
Elles se laissaient enivrées,
Emporter par le tourbillon.

tr. G.B.

49. SOLDIERS' CHORUS

(The Decembrists—1941)

The 'Decembrists' were the first Russians to plan an active revolt against the tyranny of their rulers. On 14 December 1825 they assembled to demonstrate during a military parade in St Petersburg (now Leningrad). They hoped that the troops in the parade (who march in to this song) would support them but it did not work out that way and, in fact, the crowds were cruelly fired upon at the order of the panic-stricken Czar. The music is by Yuri Shaporin.

On - ward, on - ward. e - ver_ on - ward,
On - ward, on - ward. e - ver_ on - ward,

March - ing on - ward o'er the plain,_ in - to bat - tle,
March - ing on - ward o'er the plain,_ Hearts are stea - dy,

in - to _ bat - tle go our gal - lant fight - ing men.
sa - bres _ rea - dy: on to meet the Turk a - gain.

Eh in the _ gar - den, in the gar - den stands a - lone _
Eh tears are _ fall - ing, heads are shy - ly turned a - side._

my be - lov - ed, my _ be - lov - ed. Sad - ly she _ must
Do not weep for me _ my _ dar - ling. I'll come back to

stay at home. I'll come back to take my bride._____
take my bride.

tr. G.B.

50. JOHNNIE CRACK and THE MILKMAID'S SONG

(Under Milk Wood—1947)

A little scene from Dylan Thomas's famous play, showing children playing in the street while the choir practises nearby. These two songs, which fit so neatly together, are by Daniel Jones.

84

D.C. to 'Johnnie Crack', then Male voices start 'What a dainty life' again on second beat of the 'All Children' bar.

85

THE GUITAR

(*a*) Strumming with the thumb and picking the separate notes of the chord in harp fashion (suitable for slow or medium-paced songs).

(*b*) The most useful technique for rhythmic accompaniment is the alternation of thumb and first finger. The thumb (T) plucks the bottom note of the chord, and the first finger flicks down across the remaining strings with the nail (N). An additional beat can be introduced by coming back up the strings with the pad (P) of the first finger.

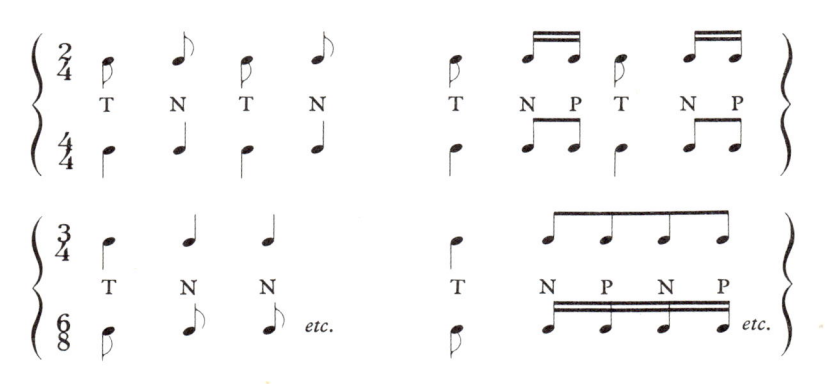

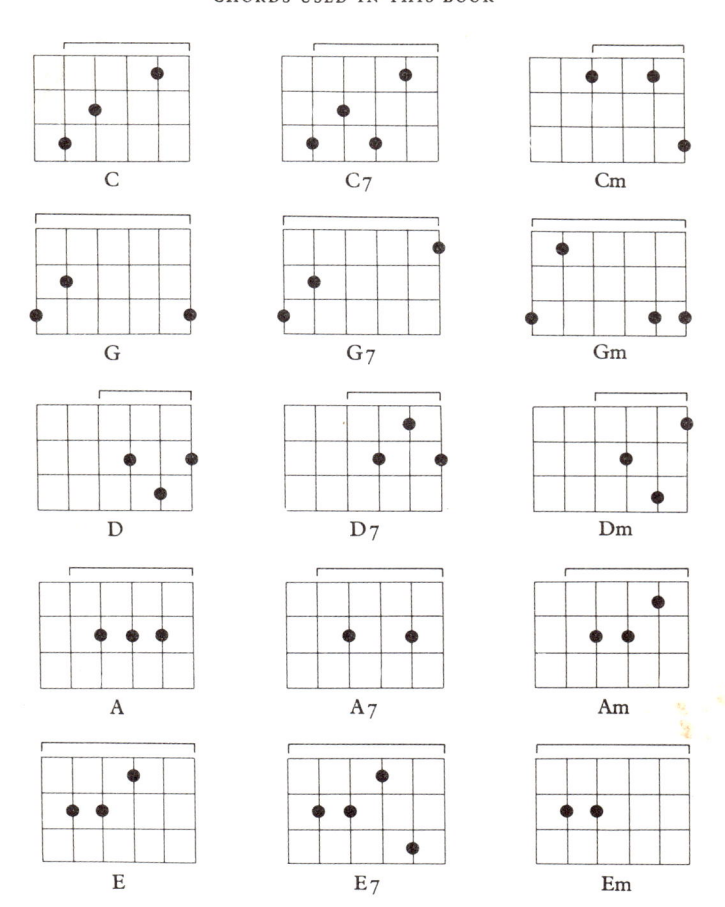

C   C7   Cm

G   G7   Gm

D   D7   Dm

A   A7   Am

E   E7   Em

⌐‾‾‾‾⌐ Strings to be used.

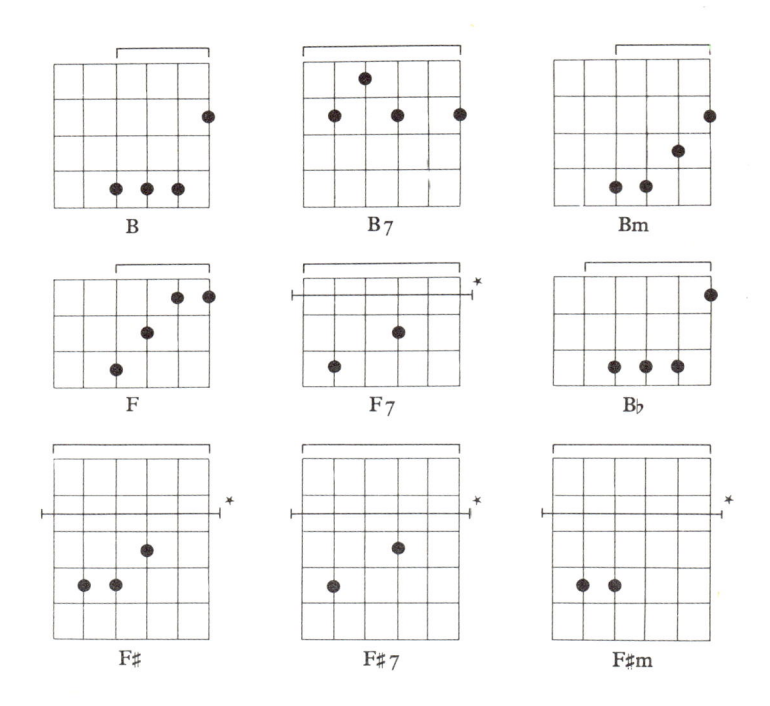

* Place first finger across all strings.

⌐──┐ Strings to be used.

BIBLIOGRAPHY

BOOKS OF SONGS

English Folksongs, collected by Cecil Sharp (Centenary Edition): Novello.
The Penguin Book of English Folksongs, by A. L. Lloyd and R. Vaughan Williams.
English County Songs, by Lucy Broadwood: Cramer.
A Garland of English Folksongs, by Frank Kidson: Ascherberg.
A Jubilee Book of English Folksongs, by Imogen Holst: O.U.P.
A Dorset Book of Folksongs, by B. Kindersley and J. Brocklebank: O.U.P.
Shuttle and Cage, by Ewan MacColl: Workers' Music Association.
Scotland Sings, by Ewan MacColl: Workers' Music Association.
The Singing Island, by Ewan MacColl and Peggy Seeger: Mills Music.
Folk Songs of North America, by Alan Lomax: Cassell.
Folk Songs of Europe, by M. Karpeles: Novello.
Fifty Russian Folksongs, by E. L. Swerkoff: Novello.
Music Sounds Afar: Follett Publications Inc.
Mélodies populaires, by J. Tiersot: United Music Publishers (separately or in four
    volumes).
Songs and Shanties from the Seven Seas, by Stan Hugill: Routledge, Kegan & Paul.
American Favourite Songs, by Pete Seeger: Oak Publications Inc., N.Y.

BOOKS ABOUT SONG

The Singing Englishman, by A. L. Lloyd: Workers' Music Association.
English Folk Song, by Cecil Sharp: O.U.P.
Sing a Song of England, by Reginald Nettel: Phoenix.
The Idiom of the People, by James Reeves: Heinemann.
The Everlasting Circle, by James Reeves: Heinemann.
The Broadside Ballad, by Leslie Sheppard: Herbert Jenkins.

REFERENCE BOOKS

English Folksongs of the Appalachian Mountains (2 vols.), by Cecil Sharp: O.U.P.
English and Scottish Popular Ballads, by F. J. Child: Folklore Press, U.S.A.: O.U.P.
Traditional Tunes of the Child Ballads, by B. H. Bronson: Princeton U.P.

INSTRUMENTAL TUTORS

American Folk Guitar, by Alan Lomax and Pete Seeger: Robbins Music.
How to Play the Five-string Banjo, by Pete Seeger: Topic Records (with records).

RECORD LIST

The following are recordings of songs in this book:

Turpin Hero—Melodisc, EPM7-112 (Steve Benbow).
Jesse James—H.M.V., CLP1192 (Alan Lomax).
The Gresford Disaster—Topic, 10T13 (Ewan MacColl).
On a British Submarine—H.M.V., CLP1362 (Cyril Tawney).
The Fox—Brunswick LA8583 (Burl Ives).
Mrs McGrath—Collector, JEI4 (Dominic Behan).
Mrs Hooligan's Christmas Cake—Collector, JEI1 (Dominic Behan).
The Fireman's not for me—H.M.V., DLP1204 (Shirley Bland and Jimmy MacGregor).
Jamaica Farewell—Nixa, 7N25021 (Nina and Frederik).
Dirty old Town—Collector, JEB1 (Benbow Folk Four).
Fourpence a Day—Topic, 10T13 (Ewan MacColl).
I've been working on the Railroad—Capitol, P8324 (Roger Wagner Chorale).
Whaling in Greenland—Collector, JEB1 (Benbow Folk Four).
The Calton Weaver—H.M.V., CLP1327 (Jimmy MacGregor).
Fine Girl you are—H.M.V., CLP1362 (Seamus Ennis).

Many more interesting folk-songs will be found on these records, and on other recordings by th above companies and artists.

The Marriage of Figaro—Columbia, 33CX1007-9
Der Freischütz—Decca, LXT2597-9.
La Traviata—Columbia, 33CX1370-1.
Carmen—H.M.V., ALP1762-4.
Carmen (orchestral suite)—Decca, ACL9.
The Soldiers' Chorus (*The Decembrists*)—Columbia sel 1605.
Under Milk Wood—Argo, RG21-22.